You Are "Energy", Be Energized

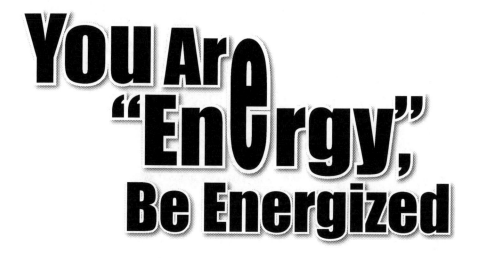

You Are "Energy," Be Energized

Charles Fletcher

authorHOUSE®

AuthorHouse™ LLC
1663 Liberty Drive
Bloomington, IN 47403
www.authorhouse.com
Phone: 1-800-839-8640

Published by AuthorHouse 01/17/2014

ISBN: 978-1-4918-5433-4 (sc)
ISBN: 978-1-4918-5432-7 (e)

Library of Congress Control Number: 2014901234

From the Author

This Book is a sequel to my first Book "The Shocking", all of my writings are written in a Non-Traditional style so that my audience can digest what is being said more easily and quickly. There by shocking the consciousness of those that reads it, rather they believe it or not. I do not believe in giving the readers a long diatribe on a subject that takes only a few words to get the point across. I think the readers would appreciate reading something that is clear and to the point without a long drawn out story that would take you around the world to express the thought. I am very blunt about the things I research and write about, the fact of the matter is that "Energy" gives us the ability to think and to think wisely. I think very deeply about the things I write about. I pick and choose the top-pics based on what I see and feel. Like twitter, you can say what you want in a sentence or paragraph to send a message; I have chosen short articles for my message.

Thank You Sincerely,

Charles Fletcher

About the Title

The title of my Book "You Are "Energy" Be Energized" is taken from a real deep, deep sense of meditation. Most people will meditate differently and rightly so. Oprah Winfrey and Deepak Chopra both teamed up and produced a meditation CD. They felt a need to teach the public about meditation, and how it can affect your whole life, Then there are the properties of meditation such as which direction you choose to take once you begin to meditate and go into a deep trans. As I meditate I try writing things as I see them. When we meditate, it is that "Energy" within us that causes our minds to focus. It is "Energy" that holds the power for all of our thoughts, as "Energy" is the archives of all history and knowledge. Your "Energy" gives you the ability to choose the directions you want to go once you are in a deep Trans of meditation; you might choose to travel back in time to visit your ancestors centuries of years gone by, because with "Energy" time does not exist and there is no such thing as time. Should you choose to advance forward, your "Energy" will guide you to thoughts greater than you can ever imagine. Please remember that "Energy" is everything and everything is "Energy" all weather related functions are the arsenals of "Energy". Nevertheless you should be very careful of what you think about. Most religions believe that God controls "Energy" and God is another name for "Energy", they also believe that the soul, the spirit, the mind are separate entities from God but they are all one and the same. "Energy" has been known by many names throughout centuries, however, when the smoke clears at the end of the day "Energy" has always been, will always be the dominate controlling force in all life and in all Creation. Have you ever ask yourself what is the purpose of life here on planet earth and why were we chosen to be here? Life exist throughout all of Creation because "Energy" is life and life is "Energy" and "Energy" is everywhere in this vast Universe and in all Creations and beyond. I continue to look at the equality in human life and cannot fine this equality. Does this mean that some people are better than others? Yes, it sparks the question as to why many have wealth and others do not. Does equal opportunity make you equal to the next person?

Not necessarily, every human that was missioned here was sent for a purpose, some missions appear to duplicate others but they are all slightly different in scope. As complex as "Energy" is we must take a closer look at the elements that help formulate the purpose of each individual mission. When we look at positive thoughts and negative thoughts are they equal in scope? Of course not and each of these must balance the other in scope, If the human mind("Energy") is not balanced, the spirit or soul is not balanced, so how can two individuals be equal? Wealth is only one factor for determining equality, your economic status is what determines equality in today's world and there is always someone richer or poorer than you rather mentally and physically. Death is something most people do not like to talk about, nevertheless, death is another component of "Energy" and death is just like a stop light or stop sign after you have stopped then your "Energy" goes again to some other place or environment we call the next dimension. Everything your body has concurred will come to an abrupt halt, your body stops breathing and all your "Energy" leaves your body and after that "Energy" travels someplace else, this is undetermined because of this vast creation and there are other "Energies" waiting for your return. This is why I tell my audience that your death is not the first death you have experienced, Death signifies that it is time to move from one destination to the next destination. Your "Energy" is a traveler and you made a brief stop on the planet earth as part of your mission, Your Elders will determine your next destination. When my time here expires there will be someone coming behind me to take up the same cause of action, this "Energy" or person will be greater in scope and more powerful than me. That is the way it has always been and it works because this is how change evolves. The next person will have a greater task, you might not like what they do but that is their mission. So . . . where is the equality? Nevertheless, President Barack Obama himself has quoted the "Bill of Rights" written by slave owners, men that thought they could bring equality to a world of madness, saying that: "All men are created equal. How are we created equal and it is not because we are human, we could not excel if we were all equal, nothing is equal in Creation. No one, absolutely no one can ever explain the meaning of equality.

Thereby, we are dedicating this book to all Public and Private schools of thought and to all Scientist, Religious and Political leaders.

Creative writing deals with the in-depth thought and research into your own mind as it relates to human thought waves rather in politics, religion or science. Most of us do not realize how the thought process began in the human brain and how the thoughts are transmitted from "Energy" to the brain, we will discuss this more later on in our presentation. However, we begin with all religions as they will all justify their teaching with scriptural events. I cannot say enough about in-depth thinking in politics and religion because most people will not venture beyond the present day conversation as their daily pattern of thinking. Religion and politics is the language of today and if you follow both of these practices you will see that neither will never, ever talk about the environmental effects of "Energy". Absent of environmental education and the functions of the elements, you are no less just talking to the wind with no substance. There are billions of people trying to understand the true meaning of politics and religion, yet they settle for the same continuous reading in scriptural philosophy, theology and political science. Most people cannot recognize change when it comes they are clueless and locked into their own mode of thinking, they want the same knowledge, the same thinking with no change and if there are any changes it has to be consistent with yesterday's biblical teachings and philosophy. Religion and politics are always the same. With politics in America they rely on the United States Constitution and the laws that support it. Religion in America relies on the same politics and principles and they both work hand in glove with each other. There are over 4,000 religions worldwide and they all are saying the same thing, the only thing different about them are the languages. There is always a miraculous birth; someone is always rising from the dead, God is always a gender mostly male, and the gender is the Creator of all life. This is being repeated constantly and the people that believe this is always locked and trapped in a Pandora's Box with superstitious beliefs. Money being the influence in both religion and politics are the controlling sources as to what is being said in the social media. These rich individuals with unlimited resources keep the masses in a state of docility and ignorance not knowing what is going on from day to day.

Table of Contents

Racism with the Rich and Wealthy Slave Masters 1

What is the Purpose of Life? 2

As a Human, We must Stand Up, Grow Up, Wake Up, Wise Up 4

Our United States Constitution Must be Re-Written............................... 6

High Power Intelligence=The Atom.. 7

No Congressional Employee Should be Paid for Doing Nothing............... 8

Congressional Fund Raising & Hand Gun Violence 9

Special Report on Hubris=War Crimes and High Treason 10

The Many Neck names of "Energy"... 11

The Hypocritical Oak of the United States Congress 12

Thinking for Yourself.. 13

Stand Up for Truth... 14

Response to Your Message From President Obama 15

Response to the Presidents Letters 18

Environmental Education Trumps Religion.. 19

The Word God and Truth are Concepts and are not Facts. 20

What is Faith? 21

What Does It Mean To Change? 22

The Meaning of Worship.. 23

Children in a Play Pin 24

What Is It That Controls Your Thinking? 25

Media Control 26

The Universe and the Big Bang Theory.. 27

What is Marriage and What Does It Mean?... 28

All Religions Have Run Amuck.. 29

"Energy" Heals and "Energy" Kills 30

Why the Clergy Keep Taking Parishioners Around and
Round in Circles? 31

New World Order Plan to Kill 90% of the World Population 33

Environmental Education is the Highest Knowledge in Creation 34

We the People of The United States 35

Quantum Physics 36

OUT-OF-SIGHT, OUT-OF-MIND 37

Environmental Education Is Absent From the Curriculum
of Knowledge 38

We Cannot Advance To Our Future by Cling to Our Past 39

Government Shutdown is Equal to Extortion and Blackmail 41

Here is a Fact that Can Never be Disputed 44

Communication is the Highest Educational form of
Teaching in all Creation 45

Domestic Violence is a Serious Health Hazard 46

Are We Truly Robotic Creatures? 47

Politics & Religion is the worse forms of Enslavement 48

The Power of Creation 50

Nothing in all Creation can move without the Power of "Energy" 51

Female of the First Power in Human Creation 52

When the Mind Entertains Garbage it Becomes Addicted to That
Garbage 53

A Typhon and Hurricane is One and The Same 54

All Men are "NOT" Created Equal 55

The Woman is The Kunapha, The High Priestess 56

Racism with the Rich and Wealthy Slave Masters

The election is over but what were the lessons we learned from the re-election of President Barack Obama? Let us take a short review of the Republican Party's attempt to demonize the President and make it appear as if the President was producing negative politics with his commercials when it was Mitt Romney, Carl Rove and the Republicans that were constantly interjecting the negative press. Just look at how Mitch McConnell along with those rich and wealthy donors like Donald Trump, the Koch Brothers etc. Even with all their wealth they still could not stop the President from winning the re-election. It was the President and the remarkable "Energy for change that he put forth for his re-election. This is what happens when you conform to the natural idea for change, because we began to flow with the change of natural "Energy". But let us take this a step further, This has been the same practice with the religious right. The so-call God that all religious denominations worship has been the Rich and Wealthy Slave Masters of the World. They love being worshiped for something they never done. Just as Mitt Romney was making things up and lying as he tried to win the election, This was the same principal and tactic with the Rich and Wealthy in ancient times gone by. They also knew that the masses were a gullible people and many would never question the religious philosophy of the Rich because they were known as the God of all people. The word God and its terminology never existed but was made up and invented by the Rich and Wealthy Slave Masters of the World.

What is the Purpose of Life?

We have completed the manuscript for the publishing of our book ***"The Shocking"*** , which is in print as we speak. it should be released around the first of the year and we will keep you posted as to when and what book stores will carry it. There is also a second book in the works. As a focus point, we need to look at what is truly happening to our society world wide. Most people still does not seem to understand what "Energy" is and it's purpose and function. 90 % of the world population does not understand the function of "Energy'. When a hurricane, tornado, earth quake, tsunami, thunder, lightening, rain, snow, heat or cold, they always think that it is God that causes these thing to happen. Here is a hard truth, when a person has been tricked all of his/her life into thinking that religion is going to save them from something after their death has swallowed the biggest lie ever told., the larger question is, ***"What are you being saved from"?*** "Energy" is life ever lasting. Your physical body is nothing more than a vessel that is controlled by the "Energy" within each and every one of us. At the time of your death, "Energy" will exits from the body and reunite with other "Energies" that surround you at the time of your death. Why do you think this knowledge was never taught to us? The whole idea was to keep the world masses as perpetual slaves. Money have brain wash the masses in thinking that if you have money, this is all you need to succeed. When you see these churches, Mosques, synagogues, entertainers, athletes and the rich slaves masters with luxurious homes, cars jewelry and other material wealth as a mean to show you what money can buy and at the same time it is to antagonize your mind and thinking that you need more money to live a successful life. ***So the religious spirituality in many forms are extremely deceptive, All religious functions reguardless of the denomination are about how much money they can obtain from the masses, just Look what the Republican Party done in the November election? They thought they could buy the Office of the President, but they fail. This has been going on for centuries, they make things up as they go. The same thing is how religion works?*** You can not point to nothing in creation not one single thing that "Energy" did not create. NOTHING! It controls both the negative and the positive. So why is it that the rich worship money? The purpose of life is to study creation and utilize the best of the "Energy" within us. Our "Energy" is the real life we seek, it controls what we see, the eye is only a vehicle for "Energy", same thing with your nose, ear, throat etc. We will look at what the next dimension for tale us as we raise our consciousness to higher level.

As a Human, We must Stand Up, Grow Up, Wake Up, Wise Up

If you listen to a radio what is it you hear? Voices, music, sounds of pleasure to the ears and many times the music makes the body feel good and jubilant causing the body to move and dance. When you watch television you are watching not only a picture in motion but you are also listening to the voices of live television rather the people you see are actors or news casters. However, bottom line is that both scenarios is an indication as to how "Energy" is the center of all technology. The Voices you here is "Energy" coming from other "Energies" that have "Energized the produces you see and use to make your conveyance more comfortable, that is the Television and radio. It is "Energy" that created all that you can imagine this also include the negative and positive influences of "Energy".

As a man or woman we must first man up, woman up, stand up, grow up, wake up and wise up to our own level of consciousness we must first awaken the consciousness within which is that "Energy" that you see and hear inside of you, once that consciousness has been awaken then comes the understanding as to the many dimensions of creation. How do you go about seeking other dimension? The first thing we must learn is to look at the elements and what they can teach us about our own dimension because it is the elements that create each and every thing we can see in Creation. We can began with the atoms, neutrons, electrons, protons, isotopes, carbons etc. Protons, neutrons both make up the atomic mass of all elements. ***Protons are the positive charge,*** the ***Neutrons are the negative charge*** to the nucleus by which the electrons is where ***they both*** reside. When you are able to see what "Energy" does, you will want to understand what "Energy" is created from, that is ***helium, atoms and hydrogen*** are the ***basic elements***. among other elements in the creation of "Energy".

Let us take a look at the negative components of "Energy", like gun violence in communities, today in the news, there was another school shooting

4

where 18 students and 9 adults a total of 27 dead including the shooter. in a elementary school was kill along with the shooter's mother who was also a teacher at the same school in Newtown Connecticut. Prior to the re-election of President Obama, his critics, the Republican Party has indicated that if President was re-elected that he would take away your guns. With the assault weapon on the street, ***The President and Congress need to take away all gun nation wide***. In China and many other countries guns are not allowed in communities. A person that are trained in Marshall arts has a lethal weapon just as a boxer. But in America it is the NRA (National Rifle Association) that has put fear into the minds of the people that the second Amendment protects the people right to bear arms.

Years ago we requested at a meeting with the United States Environmental Protection Agency to place a monitoring system in each and every community that could monitor all elements that moves around all people just as the weather bureau monitors the pollen in the air. With this type of system communities would be able to track and follow the negative elements that may have an impact on violence in all communities. It is the elements in the environment that causes violence in human behavior in all communities. The EPA told us that this would be too costly.

Our United States Constitution Must be Re-Written

Mr. President:

With all the trouble you are having with Congress, the debt, the massacre in Connecticut, the war in Afghanistan, the selection of a new Secretary of State, The assault weapons ban, and gun violence etc. It appears to look like you have your arms full. This also raises the question concerning the (Re-Write of the United States Constitution). ***Please do not say we have the Amendments, "NO," Mr. President, we are still utilizing that same doctrine and contents of the United States Constitution as a protected document.*** We cannot continue to enforce the contents of that document on the people that was written in 1776 and allow this same document to apply to the people in 2012. ***For Example, the 2nd Amendment to the Constitution, "the right to bear arms", was for the Military not for the common people, what happen? This is also worth mentioning that the Founding Father had indicated that the Constitution should be Re-written every 20 years, Why haven't it been re-written?*** The Rich did not want it to be re-written . . . Remember what you told Mitt Romney, when his statements caused you to tell him, ***"We use to use bayonets and ride horses but today we ride in cars and use Submarines",*** this suggest that time has passed and the laws in the past is not applicable to today's times. ***This is the right opportunity and time to change the Constitution and make it applicable to the time we are living in today***. This is why the Republicans want to go back to the "Good Old' Boy days, they don't want to change nor re-write the Constitution because it satisfy their greedy needs to keep the people enslaved. This is a necessity rather than an afterthought. Mr. President you cannot continue to submit to whims of the Rich Republican Party. There is a demand that the American People be protected from this insidious on slaughter of mayhem and carnage of our children.

High Power Intelligence=The Atom

If we continue to hold on to this money hungry, money grabbing society, we will loose the true focus of our mission. ***What is the our true mission?*** Let us take a real close look at the "elements" in creation, these tiny macroscopic particulates are the controlling source of all existence. The "Atom", a tri-circular system and movement that provides us with a complex system with magnetic energy that has the ability to galvanize other elements and produce new creations unlimited. The "Atom" is one of the sources of "Energy" along with hydrogen and helium that creates a more powerful force. However, if we observe the bigger picture like planets, stars and galaxies etc. We see volumes of particulate matter in clusters all over the universe, we conclude that the "Atom" is utilized in each and every created thing. There by "Energy" must be the source of all created matter. Should we continue to focus our attention on money and religion we loose the ability to rise up from the state of ignorance that have and will continue to hold us back like a heavy stone tied to our neck that has been thrown to the bottom of a vast ocean with no one there to help. We continue to look at our financial situation and rightfully so because we have families and responsibilities, but we seem to neglect the energy within us that can change our status and our way of life. Here is what we seem to mis-understand about the use of the word "GOD" this terminology was invented by the Rich and Wealthy Slave Masters centuries ago to teach the masses who had the real power in society. Here in the United States, all American money has ***"In God We Trust"*** written and embossed on it. This is the real God that the Rich believe in. Look at what is happening in the United States Congress, The Republican Party, they want a tax cut for the Rich on the backs of the poor and middle class, why? Because they see themselves as the GOD. They feel that they are entitled to do this because that has been their way for centuries.

No Congressional Employee Should be Paid for Doing Nothing

Mr. President:

It truly appears that the Republicans Party has refused to work with you and the American People. It would seem to me that when some one is employed by the Federal Government and they refuse to do their job, then they should not be paid a salary based on the work that is required of them. ***Secondly, the American People need to know the job description of the United States Congress so that if they refuse to do the job they are sworn to do This is like they are being paid for doing NOTHING, they should not be paid for something they are not doing. The American People are being short changed by the United States Congress and the Republican Party.*** Mr. President you cannot continue this charade knowing they are violating their Oath of Office. Should you stop their pay checks you will start getting better results, they are employed by the American People which is the Federal Government, they don't believe in paying their debt so what are you going to do? ***Salaries for the United States Congress Should not be Paid for work not Done.***

Congressional Fund Raising & Hand Gun Violence

Mr. President:

As we shared with you in our last memo, you cannot continue this charade knowing that the Congress are violating their Oath of Office. Should you stop their pay checks you will start getting better results, they are employed to do the peoples business and not do their own personal business by doing fund raising during the same time they should be working on the peoples business such as the Bills you have put before the Congress. Should you fine any of the Congressional employees doing fun raising on the Peoples Time, They should be fined and their pay should be suspended and if they raising funds on the Governments time their pay should be suspended, ***All money that is raised during this time they should be working on the peoples business those funds by right should be given to the Federal Government because they are raising funds on the Governments time and not working on the Peoples business. Salaries for the United States Congress Should not be Paid for work not Done.***

Mr. President, you continue to look at a band on assault weapons yet the murder of Hadiya was done with a hand gun, therefore how can you justify the assault weapons band when 95 percent of all killing are done with a hand gun? Here is what I think, ***(all guns are assault weapons when looking at the power of a fire arm)***. You made it clear on Friday that in comparing the shootings in 2012 on a national bases is equivalent to a massacre every four months. However, Mr. President the killing by most gang members are done with a hand gun. Secondly, gang members obtain guns without a criminal back ground check. In fact, gang members don't do criminal back ground checks. So what is the point? They purchase guns from dealers and underground manufactures.

Additionally, Senator John McCain is a man that needs to be accountable for what he say. He is a senior citizen that needs to be find each time he makes a false statement against the President of the United States.

Special Report on Hubris=War Crimes and High Treason

Mr. President:

In view of the MSNBC Rachel Meadow Special last night "The Hubris" Selling the Iraq war, I find these facts as evidence of a Conspiracy to overthrow the United States Government and war crimes at the highest level. **_Both George W. Bush, Richard Chenney and Donald Rumsfel along with certain other Cabinet members of the George W. Bush Administration all are guilty of War Crimes and High Treason in violation of Title 18 USC Criminal Code._** Mr. President, it is inconceivable to think that these individuals would devise a conspiracy to go to war knowing that a fabricated lie was used to over throw Saddam Hussain and ultimately caused him to be put to death knowing he had nothing to do with the attack on 9/11, nor was there ever found chemical or biological weapons of mass destruction. The death and murder of thousands of Iraq people along with American troops that was innocently killed not ever knowing the real truth as to why they were sent there in the first place.

These men must be brought to trail for their criminal acts of Treason and War Crimes against the United States without justification. **_Mr. President, in good conscious you can not portray yourself as the President of change and allow a vast conspiracy of this magnitude to go unpunished on behalf of the American People? In truth Mr. President it does not matter how many bills you get through Congress, the Bush Administrations acts of injustice is on your watch and should you allow this injustice to escape the laws of justice for the American People, they will surely label you as a co-conspirator of these acts of War Crimes and HighTreason because of your failure to bring justice for the American People and the People of Iraq._** It is obvious why Senator John McCain and the GOP and many Democratic Congressmen act in the manner they do toward you, they see you as a weak President that fears reprisle from the Rich Slave Masters of the world. I think Dr. King said it best: **_"If you don't stand for something, you will fall for anything"._**

The Many Neck names of "Energy"

The many neck names of "Energy" is: God, Allah, Elohim, Elaha, Ehyeh, Makuru etc. There are so many neck names until there is not enough space to name them. For centuries the general public has used many neck names to discribe the workings of "Energy" and for many religious believers this takes on a whole different meaning. A neck name may be derive from or related to what the person is well known for. A reputation, a term of endearment describing; a person or inanimate object for which the speaker or individual feels love or affection describing a divine personage. For example, in the Christians religion they believe that the nature of God is a mystery.

The Hypocritical Oak of the United States Congress

Have any one notice that no matter how heard President Obama try to rectify the serious issues with the United States Congress with today's political fury, it always tend to fall on its face. Yet these are token religious believers. This is what religion does to the minds of those who practice the religious doctrine. On one hand they claim that God is on America's side because America is a righteous nation and on the other hand they claim that America is the greatest nation on earth with the gtreatest Army on earth. If this was true, Why would George Bush, Dick Cheney and Donald Rumsfeld violated their own Oath of Office? It really appears that the more the Country talks about religion, and politics, the deeper the country go's into a negative frenzy on all issues. The President has limited options when it comes to getting things done because the GOP refuse to support the President on any issue. So let me ask the question, If the United States Congress are true religious followers of the Bible, where is it in the Bible that gives them the authority to practice racism and bigotry against the President of The United States? Unless the whole objective of writing the Bible was to promote this type of behavior. The more they claim that God is on their side the deeper they go into the negative behavior of racism and bigotry ,lead by those that believe in God, Jesus and the Christian concept of religion. So What is the alternative and objective of this madness? This kind of behavior increases recidivism, bigotry and violence at the highest level of government and it keeps violence at a high pitch around the nation. How do we bring this madness to an end? If we believe in total change, we must stop religious bigotry and racism. We must put an end to these adulterous religions that impels the people from acting responsible.

Thinking for Yourself

Check this out, over 99 percent of the world's population loves for some one else to do their thinking for them. This has always been the idea of the Rich and Wealthy White Slave Masters because it was their idea for the slaves to be dependent upon the master. So what did the master do to perpetuate this type of thinking? They brought in religion, you see it does not matter what kind of religion you practice the dependency is always there, the dependency is either on your lord and savior Jesus Christi or it is on God. If the religion is Islam it is on Muhammad or Allah etc. They will depend upon the Bible or the Quran etc., in religion they are always depending on what the Slave Masters has taught them from generation to generation never breaking the chain of succession. Case in point the Billionaire Bill Gates was on 60 minutes on Sunday telling the world how he had purchased all the rights to all of Leonardo Advance's documents because Deviance's ideas were tantamount to today's time and circumstances. Bill Gate has design a toile as a sanitation unit for people with HIV-Aids that could flush without conventional pluming. This $68 Billion dollar computer giant and his wife are helping thousands of HIV-AIDS victims in Africa. But that is not the kicker, hears is the point, that same "Energy" that Deviance had is the same "Energy" we have today and has elevated the ideas of millions far greater than Deviance. Just ask Bill Gates. But the whole idea for the Rich and Wealthy Slave Masters of today is to continue the dream of keeping the slaves docile and dependent. "Energy" controls all thinking in each and every human thought, nothing in Creation is Greater than "Energy". ABSOLUTLY NOTHING!

Stand Up for Truth

It takes strong and powerful courage to stand up for truth, most people can't stand up at all because they are to afraid what others will say about what think to be facts. Common sense tells you curtain things that are factual in nature and can not be refuted. However, as someone told me recently," common sense is not common any more". If you do not believe as others believe, the as part of their medical curriculum. will consider you as hypocritical to those things they have grown up to believe as true. They love to take the easy way out, they are afraid to challenge their own thinking utilising their own inter "Energy". If you tell them that the use of a computer is all "Energy" connected, there will always be someone there to say that is not true. But you can't rely on those that cannot see your interest. You most move on to that next level of understanding until they can understand that persons point of view. In my book the "Shocking" I talked about the enter self and there are many that do not understand the concept of the enter self. Some told me that they rely on their doctor for advice and dependency; even doctors do not have environmental education to properly diagnosis a particular illness because environmental education was never required as a curriculum in their medical education. Don't take my word, research it for yourself.

Response to Your Message From President Obama

Dear Charles:

Thank you for writing. Few challenges are more urgent than climate change, and I appreciate your perspective.

For the sake of our children and our future, we must do more to combat climate change. Its effects, including warmer temperatures, extreme weather, and sea level rise, are already being felt across our Nation and around the world. The 12 hottest years on record have all come in the last 15. Heat waves, droughts, wildfires, and floods are all increasingly frequent and intense. We can choose to believe that these disasters are the result of coincidence, or we can accept the overwhelming judgment of science and act before it is too late. Our planet's future depends on a global commitment to permanently reduce the greenhouse gas pollution causing climate change.

In my first year in office, I set a goal of significantly reducing greenhouse gas emissions by 2020. Today, my Administration's actions have helped drive down our carbon emissions to their lowest level in nearly two decades. We are now on a path to a cleaner and more secure energy future—but there is still more work to be done.

Changing the way we produce and use energy is essential to protecting our environment for future generations. To decrease our dependence on oil and cut pollution, my Administration has established the toughest new fuel economy standards in history. These standards will double the fuel efficiency of our cars and light trucks by the middle of the next decade, saving families money at the pump while slashing harmful carbon pollution. Our Nation is becoming a global leader in advanced vehicles, and auto dealers are selling more hybrid vehicles than ever before. I am calling on Congress to use some of our oil and gas revenues to fund an Energy Security Trust that will drive new research and technology to shift our cars and trucks off oil for good. The Trust will support research into a range of cost-effective technologies, including advanced vehicles that run on electricity, homegrown biofuels, and domestically produced natural gas.

Thanks in part to my Administration's investments in clean energy—the largest of their kind in American history—the United States has doubled renewable energy generation from wind, solar, and geothermal sources, and tens of thousands of Americans now have jobs as a result. I also set a goal to double renewable electricity production again by 2020 to build on our momentum and create even more jobs. The United States military—the largest energy consumer in the world—is reducing its fuel use and improving its operational performance through a historic commitment to clean energy.

We must lead the world in developing the technology and driving the innovation that will power tomorrow's industries and jobs. Congress must come together to pursue a bipartisan, market-based solution to climate change. This should not be a divisive issue—it is one in which the best interests of our planet and the well-being of our economy are fundamentally aligned. I have repeatedly called on Congress to stop giving away $4 billion a year in oil and gas subsidies to an industry that has never been more profitable, and instead to pass clean energy tax credits to cultivate a market for innovation in clean energy technology in the United States. And if Congress does not act soon to reduce pollution and speed the transition to more sustainable sources of energy, I am prepared to take executive action.

As we work to reduce our own emissions and build resilience to climate change, we must also forge solutions that ensure other countries do the same. My Administration led international climate negotiations that produced the first national greenhouse gas reduction commitments by major developed and developing countries, the most robust transparency system for reviewing commitments to date, and historic global climate resiliency efforts. At the same time, we have worked through a range of international initiatives, including through the G-20, for the global phase-out of inefficient fossil fuel subsidies around the world. The threat posed by climate change is not confined within the borders of any country, and our response must continue to be global.

Finally, we must take action to prepare our communities for the consequences of climate change. Through the Climate Change Adaptation Task Force launched by my Administration in 2009, Federal agencies have developed first-ever initiatives to ensure our communities, economy, infrastructure, and natural resources are resilient in the face of extreme weather and other impacts of climate change. We are also helping increase the preparedness and resilience of American communities by providing actionable scientific information and technical assistance to cities and towns that are already feeling the impacts of rising seas, more severe storms, and other effects of climate change.

We must summon the spirit of optimism and the willingness to tackle tough problems that led previous generations to meet the challenges of their times. My Administration is making a serious, sustained commitment to address climate change, and I encourage you to learn more about our efforts at <u>www. WhiteHouse.gov/energy/climate-change</u>.

Thank you, again, for writing.

Sincerely,

Barack Obama

Response to the Presidents Letters

Thank you Mr. President:

You have indeed: responded to something dear to my heart, "Environmental "Energy" and Climate Change is so sad to know that the majority of the world population does not understand the meaning of globe" Climate Change and this include The United States Congress. Climate change is an atmospheric change in the four seasons of each year, this is caused by the realignment of the Planets or what is called the "Time period" which imitates a change in the weather, a change in the speed of the planets, a change in human behavior, a change in the way we think about the climate we live in. There are negative and positive changes in the atmosphere these changes have to be balanced and "Energy" is the equal Librium by which these changes will take place. Nevertheless, this change has a tremendous adverse effect on human behavior and it causes many to become dysfunctional on many levels. I'm sure you have experienced many of these behaviors in your travels. The United States Congress is a prime example of serious behavior disorders. They cannot agree on simple things that are vital to interest and needs of the American people. Many cannot understand the simplicity of the use of "Energy" and it's implications. We might be looking at an entire generation retrograding back into a chattel slavery mentality. Mr. President, when you can see 95 percent of the world population constantly depending upon something other than themselves for their subsidence. They do not believe in the "Energy operating within their own body. "Energy" is the greatest Power in Creation and this knowledge has been lost in a maze of ignorance and religious beliefs. This is because environmental education was never taught in our educational system nor in the churches, mosques and synagogues.

Environmental Education Trumps Religion

Environmental Education Trumps Religion, the Entire Creation is a Chemistry & a Science Project in a living Active Motion. All Religions are manmade and Un-Natural to the Human mind.

It is impossible to look at this vast Creation and not recognize the absolute force of "Energy". Tornados, Hurricanes, Earthquakes, Volcanos, Tsunamis etc. Although the Obama Administration has pointed to "Energy" as Focal fuel, wind and solar. "Energy" is the Creator of all life and inanimate objects. How can religion be so blind? No one can deny the fact that "Energy" is the Absolute Power in Creation? The God concept originated in Africa then later the Greek God Zeus was the icon for religious beliefs . . . The Rich and Wealthy expanded this concept to include the one God concept then later added Jesus as the son of God all of this was to enslave the mind of the masses to the concept of religion.

The Word God and Truth are Concepts and are not Facts.

Most people do not understand the meaning of the word "CONCEPT". The word _Truth_ is a concept, the word _God_ is a concept, These two words are not facts. They are used to express an idea of un-natural origan. Today most people will confuse truth with fact, just as religious beliefs are influence by financial greed. "Money influence concepts. "There is no clear consensus of the nature of God and never has been. You always here the clergy talk about the truth and they can never explain what the truth is. They always rely on what the Bible says knowing that the Bible is full of hypocrisy, writings that other men have written centuries ago. This concept was generated by the Rich and Wealthy men of ancient times. and they are still using these same tactics today in the United States Congress. These men still utilize the United States Constitution as the document that they have taken an Oath. But their Oath does not mean anything, which contradicts what they are sworn to up hold. For starters you can not utilize a document that is hundreds of years old to address the needs of the people in the 21st century. This is what keeps the people in a docile state of confusion. It is the rich and wealthy that keeps these concepts alive. President Obama was elected by the majority of the people in the United States, but it is the "Electoral College" that selects the President".

"How crazy is that"? This is a conception that has been devised by the Rich. Most people including the United States Congress can't see the logic in this practice but refuse to try to intervene or re-write the United States Constitution. What are facts? Facts are created by the natural environment and if the individual has no environmental education and knowledge, they are totally lost from the natural world of facts.

What is Faith?

The word "FAITH" what does it mean to religious believers? *Faith is the belief in something where there is no proof or no evidence of the existence of a thing,* such as *blind faith.* Why would a person believe in something by which there is no proof? Is not this the strangest thing you have ever heard? *God and Truth are concepts and Faith is the belief in something where there is no proof or evidence.* It is clear why there are so many religions in the world, around about 250 denominations world wide. Most religions believe in a heaven and hell because this is what has influenced their belief system. *The Rich and Wealthy Slave Masters has done a wonderful job enslaving the minds of the masses, Just look at the Catholics, Muslims, Christians, Hindu, Jews etc. that believe in these religions, Then the rich makes these religions part of their everyday politics and develop laws to keep these beliefs part of a system of dysfunctional idiots.* Look at the United States Congress, this is proof as to what religion has done to the mind set of the people in America. There are more churches, mosques and synagoguesthan there are schools, colleges, universities and prions combined and the rich make sure that each one of these institutions are teaching some sort of religion because they continue to invest money into these institutions to keep them viable. *Money has always been the influence for religious beliefs. It is the rich and wealthy that keeps the religious minds going around and around in a circle of confusion but the greatest hoodwink is that the religious right keep trying to find the begining of Creation when there is no begining and there never has been a begining nor is there ever and end. Life continues to advance forward as "Energy" is the Creator of all life in Creation and it continues to Create life every fraction of a second and sooner. These religious zealous actually believe what the rich is constantly promoting like the Bible, Quran, Torah etc. This is an extremely sad day for religious believers.*

What Does It Mean To Change?

Today Attorney General Eric Holder stood up for the voting rights act, but refuse to stand up to prosecute Dick Cheney and George W. Bush. Here is what is not being said. "Energy" is what causes everything to change as this is the nature of change. Many times things change for the worse and many times it will change for the better, but we must recognize the time for change even when we disagree with that change. When there is a lack of environmental education, we are truly lost because we do not want to change. Religion has this same philosophy. The practice of any religion is to follow the teaching of the scriptures. It does not matter if the teachings are hundreds of years old just like the United States Constitution. The Rich and Wealthy wants to keep the minds of the masses enslaved to yesterday's knowledge and they do not want any changes to the scriptures or the Constitution because this keeps the resource in their control. Creation and Life is about change, as humans we must recognize change when it comes. The first and foremost change must began within the human mind which is the "Energy within you. We were all sent here to study Creation, however, what has happen to us as a people is that religion has taken the place of Environmental Education and it is extremely difficult to get the masses to understand this humongous trick-ology.

The Meaning of Worship

Have you ever looked up the word "WORSHIP" and its meaning? It means to acknowledge something beyond comprehension. Why should we worship anything beyond our comprehension? ***This is what is meant by blind faith***. When an individual prays he turns his attention inward to that power within that causes the individual to reflex on the power they call God. But God is not the entity that cause that person to lift their arms, move their feet, think their thoughts, eat their food, see that light, etc. ***"It is "Energy" that gives them that abilityy"***. *But* most people do not recognize "Energy" as the soul source of the power within their own body. Yet they know that if they had no "Energy" they could not live. Most religious zealots contribute "Energies" ability as Gods ability. God has no power over "Energy" because God never existed in the first place. A persons belief system is what bounds the individual to the concept of God never understanding why this terminology was instituted into the lexicon of words.

Children in a Play Pin

If you have ever watched a group of children in a play-pin, this is the same effect every time you watch sports on television you are watching children in a play pin. You place a ball in the play pin and it does not matter rather it is a baseball, basketball, football, Hockey punk, golf ball, kickball, and the parents are the referees. Boxing, Wrestling, horse racing, NA SCAR racing, dog racing etc. They all represent children in a play-pin. The Chicago Black hawks won the Cup and Chicago fans filled Grant Park with over 2 million fans. The night they won the Cup, the streets filled with excited fans breaking store windows, lifting barricades, drinking wildly etc. This is what fans call having fun and a good time. The Rich has placed the game of sports as a International lucrative past time and sports fanatics has boost these games as a high stakes business. These games of chance were design to influence the participant in thinking that these games are a higher form of education. They recruit these players from high schools and colleges all over the world just to get them to play and pay them enormous sum's of money. When these students graduate a great percentage will not find employment after graduation for lack of experience and if the student does not have talent, they will have to find a job working in McDonald's. Most students will never recognize the fact that they have been bamboozled into thinking that if they go to colleges they will find a better job once they complete their college education. Education was never design to find a better job, ***it was design for you find yourself intellectually.*** They never reflect the amount of money the Rich and Wealthy Slave Master has influenced the students to take out these loads and how much they must pay back with interest, this does not include their books and other fees acquired during their tenure. Just think how much those "Children In The Play-Pin" have been Hoodwinked? But ask them about climate change and what cause the storms to collide, and wait for an answer. The Rich gets Richer and the poor get poorer.

What Is It That Controls Your Thinking?

There comes a time when every human being must take a real close look at his every day thought and what it is you think about, Let us now take this up another notch. Ea.ch and every day we basically do the the same thing day in and day out. We are restricted to the places we can go either because we can not afford the transportation or the resources to go where we would like. Therefore, we look for things to pass our time, many of us look for sex, drugs, crime, mayhem, others look for sports, politics, religion etc. Most of us do not think about the Creation and what the Creation provide for our daily needs. Here is what "Environmental Education" does for "Energetic Mind". When you think about the elements that create your daily food, your thinking will retrograde to those tiny small particles that developed into this huge revolving planet and all those planets within our solar system, those galaxies, stars, meteor etc. We very seldom equate what we do every day to our future actions in the next dimension, or what we expect to acquire after we leave this dimension. Money controls our present day thoughts and controls our thinking. How can you not recognize this "Energy" that provides you with every necessity. Please keep this in mind dear people, **"Energy" does not need a God, but a God if there was one would need "Energy" in order to exist.** Those people that love to quote the bible are those who are dependent upon the words of God to save them from destruction. When Energy decides to take a life, No God can stop "Energy" from taking that life because your whole life is controlled by "Energy". You cannot think unless "Energy" gives you the power to think. Energy has the power over all life and death; there is nothing in Creation where "Energy" does not have explicit power and control over all that exist. It is "Energy" that provides all knowledge and understanding; it is the true archives of Creation.

Media Control

Most of us do not realize what Media Control is and what consist as Media. The Media is not just television, radio, cell phones and theater etc. Media is also newspapers, magazines, all books of all kind. Here again we find The Rich and Wealthy Slave Masters at the center as the controlling source of the entire media mogul empire. When the term Edit came into power as a business the editorial industry, editing became an elite source for controlling what the public could read. This has always been a source of control for the masses. When you watch T.V. the news casters reads from a cue card, so does all media out lets. Theater they read from cue cards, with news papers and magazines they edit before publication and the same with many books we read everyday. This has been going on for centuries on end. The Bible, Quran, Torah, Angil etc. was also edited by the powers of the Rich and Wealthy Slave Masters. ***By the way when we refer to the term Slave Masters we are referringto those who treat others as slaves who have no resources to protect themselves and are dependentupon the Rich for their sustenance.*** When you allow your work to be edited you are giving away your own thoughts to those that controls all media because they do not want the masses to ever wake up and find that some else is controlling their thinking. When ever you read a book in raw form with mis-spelled words out context and nothing is taken from it, that is the authors true thought unless he corrects it. Every one has typos however the editor might say: ***"Oh, these words don't make sense or it does not sound right, these are key frase's to take control of that work".*** Religion has this same philosophy, because the Rich and Wealthy also controls all religious knowledge, the clergy wants his perishers to always come to him for clarification of the religious scriptures in which he can never explain with clarity because religious scriptures has no clarity it is all media control. The movie "In My Country" with Samuel L. Jackson as a Reporter was interviewing a Apartheid Official in South Africa and the Officer told Jackson ***"The Blacks need us to control them because they are savages.*** Today in Chicago Carol Louis President of the Chicago Teachers Union said today: "The rich wants to control what our children are learning".

The Universe and the Big Bang Theory

Let us began with the word "THEORY", what is a Theory? A Theory involves no doing of itself, it is merely conjecture of something in which the individual is guessing and has no knowledge. It is a Greek terminology that has no true meaning in the universe, especially when you must deal with the natural elements in Creation such as "Energy", these facts are always clear. There is no guessing about the natural environment of the elements. When so call scientist talk about the Big Bang Theory they are really saying they do not know. Yet they continue to look for the begining of Creation. **_These are sound indications as how backward our educational system really is._** Let us look at all the so call planets in the Universe, there are so many until we can not truthfully count them because we cannot see the full circumference of the entire universe. Not only that we can not be 100 percent clear about the planets already identified by Astronomers, philanthropist and Physicist. Look at the biggest planet in our solar system Jupiter by which science say that earth could fit in the circumference of that planet some two hundred times, why have we not tried to visit that planet?. That is quite astonishing. We already know that some knid of life already exist on all of these planets because "Energy" is the Life source in Creation and "Energy" exsist within the entire Universe and it is "Energy" that cause all planets, stars and galaxies to rotate.

What is Marriage and What Does It Mean?

Today we are addressing what it means to be married. But let us first understand what marriage is, marriage is a contract between two or more individuals that feels the need to bond together for the rest of their life. However, today marriage takes on something far worse than comp animate love or conjugal love. Marriage today is an institution of rights in according to manmade laws. President Obama has indicated that Homosexuals have equal rights since the American Constitution and Bill of Rights has declared that all men are created EQUAL. ***It did not say that all women were created equal because at the time of the writing of the Bill of Rights women had no rights***, however, the "Gay Rights Activism" made it clear that women who are Gay also have equal rights as other Gay Men. Of course this does not set will in many Christen and Islamic Countries where Gay Marriage and homosexuality is punishable by death. Here in America the cost of a marriage could be from a hundred dollars to millions of dollars. Here is the kicker, what was it that causes this rift in marriage equality? It appears that homosexuality has turn into a cultural rift which is also part of our change in social society. Religion seems to restrict this marriage tie to one male and female. Procreation has always been between male and female even in the animal kingdom. Homosexual behavior is so ancient until you cannot find the beginning of this practice nowhere in history. Nevertheless, this form of behavior will alter the sexual revolution and produce another kind of human creature in creation. The change that we are embracing today causes evolutionary changes in our human behavior/culture and it will cause a transformation in the species in years to come. It is the nature of "Energy" to Create.

All Religions Have Run Amuck

The majority of the world population is not aware as to what their mission is on the planet earth. Must think that whatever they choose in life is their mission, everything in creation is based on what the elements brings to the thought process and how the individual choose which path they should take. Money is the greatest influence as to what the individual will choose. Today money is the driving force behind what we choose, how we choose and where we choose. Instead of teaching environmental education as a curriculum, religion was taught to the greater population with the use of gerrymandering, trick ology, bamboozled; hoodwink these actions contributed to millions of religious believer being led astray from the real purpose of human behavior. It does not matter what religion a person belongs to they all have the same concept. Nature is the true law of creation which gives the human being the freedom to choose. Man has developed public laws to control the material wealth of the world. When the Greek God Zeus was developed by physicists, astronomers and anthropologist they also developed the Son of Zeus and call him Jesus and pronounced (Hey-Zeus). Nevertheless, people that believe in these teachings will never, ever, never, ever question these concepts in religion. Ministers and politicians makes it almost impossible for the masses to research the real facts in creation.

They are satisfied with the illusions in the practice of religion. It does not matter what religion they believe in, they all have run amuck. Any time you teach a person that someone else died for your sins and will forgive you all your faults and in the same breath teach you "an eye for and eye" and if you are slapped on one chic you should turn the other. Just look at the racism in Trayvon Martin and Marissa Alexander cases where religion is the back bone of injustice.

"Energy" Heals and "Energy" Kills

This is the year for the people of the United States of America to elect the right person to Lead our Country to a more prosperity in the 21st century. I have received literally hundreds of emails from both political parties requesting donations because one party has raised more money than the other. Many have utilize money as the pivoting point to out spend their opponent. Using money to make more money and to high light how the rich and wealthy has prospered by using money to make more money. Debt over powering equity. President Obama must use dramatic illustrations and demonstration as to how He intends to jump start the economy and develop new employment for the unemployed, negative campaigning can over power the positive if there is no aggressive focus on change and how that change can and will help the economy. Nevertheless, those who are wide awake will support President Obama because they know what the President is trying to achieve. This election is not about who has the most money, it is about rising to the challenges of change by solving immediate problems. The change to remake America is to recognize the opposition and its failures, it taken George W. Bush 8 years to bankrupt the economy yet the opposition want the American people to think that the President must turn the economy around in four years. President Obama stated in his inauguration speech that it would take more than four years to correct the bankrupt American economy. That is not a proper balance. If the distribution of wealth is unbalance, just how can a balance in job creation would change within four years? From the beginning, Racism has dictated the posture as to the progress of President Obama. From the on set of the Obama Administration Senator Mitch McConnell has indicated that he wanted to make President Obama a one term President and for sure, the Republican Party like Rush Limbaugh has agreed that they wanted President Obama to fail. But the President has an open record of his achievements and accomplishments he has done over 75% of what he had promised the American people rather you agree or disagree. Because "Energy" is the controlling life source of all change and achievements, "Energy" will always work with the power to change rather we like it or not this is what "Energy" does. "Energy" will always bring about change to all things in life, "Energy" is Life Abundantly.

Why the Clergy Keep Taking Parishioners Around and Round in Circles?

Many people has ask me how did I become so distrustful of the belief in God? Study of the environment and creation, religion can't teach about the environment unless they teach about science. Religion will not teach about science because it is contrary to religious beliefs. I'm just going to say this before I get into my subject. When a reader begins to read Genesis in the Bible common sense should tell you that nothing can create a woman from the rib of a man, this is the biggest fabrication ever told to the senses of a human being. Out of all the births in human creation the ignorant slave is made to believe that this actually happen, knowing that every human being in his own life time was created in the womb of a woman. Parishioners in all religious beliefs are taken for a ride on a continuous bases day in and day out and the killer is they don't even know that they are being tricked. It does not matter what religion they belong to the principles are all the same. You would think after the Civil Rights Movement there would have been some safe guards in place to stop the on slaughter of bigotry with the Voting Rights Act, the whole idea of Dr. King's Dream was to march with a none violent movement to stop White Male aggression against Black People in America. Today Reverend Jesse Jackson, Reverend Al Sharpton, T.D. Jake, Minister Farrakhan and countless clergy are still doing that same old Merry-Go-Round religious teachings keeping the masses in a deeper and worse state of mind. They all are being paid millions of dollar to keep this charade going and the hurting thing is the parishioners can't even see what is happening to them. Any time you start talking to a religious individual, the only thing they can say is: "God said". Or "The Bible Said". None of them, not one of them have one clear thought of their on. They all want to be guided by thoughts of White Male aggression. When the Slave Masters told the slaves that they were free to leave the plantation, most of the slave refuse to leave because they could not think for themselves. They were use to the slave master thinking for them. This same senerio exist today because of the religious teaching, they have become dependent upon. The Slave Masters of today still has to tell them what to think and how to think by the constant feeding of religious ideas and thoughts and the slave don't want nothing else but the Bible and the none existent God that the White Slave Masters have convinced is the all powerful God, the White Slave Masters are the real God that all religions worship. Nevertheless, they can't even create a fly if all the Gods met for the purpose. Today violence has erupted worldwide and if religion had any power it could stop the violence overnight. The Rich and Wealthy Slave Masters don't want the violence to stop. If the violence stop completely worldwide this would indicate the the unification of all minds worldwide which would change the entire focus of the world economy. Why? The "Energy" of the people would solidify and change the focus of the world.

New World Order Plan to Kill 90% of the World Population

After reviewing the video of Saun Jay Guptah and Bill Gates, I am convinced that Mr. Gates and his $68,Billion Dollar Empire is helping to develop a new vaccine in Africa that will help the Secret Society under the Authority of a New World Order depopulate the whole Continent of Africa. What we said in our previous article that the White Male is the God that all religions worship and that it is the White Male that controls the wealth and resources of the entire world. Bill Gates is one of those controlling sources and he has a secret agenda that will soon expose his real intent for working in Africa, we ask that you review this video with utmost caution as he explain the use of "Energy" with a Chemistry formula. He paid $30 million dollars for all the rights of Leonardo DeVinces notes that he claim will revolutionize the world. We have sent out this video to all our colleagues and ask that you watch this video with extreme caution. You will soon see just how powerful the Rich White Male can be and there is no religion that can stop him.

Environmental Education is the Highest Knowledge in Creation

Today we will explore our next mission as a product of "Energy", but first, let us have a clear understanding as to what brought us here to the Planet Earth. If we study Creation as we should, we can clearly see that everything in creation begin with the smallest of element. These particulates are the driving force for the production of "Energy". Your human body is a product of the Earth and rightly so, your body will always remain a product of this physical earth, "Energy" created the human body as a vessel for the use of "Energy". Every single thing that move within your body is controlled by "Energy", Every organ, blood cell, bone, brain, heart muscle etc. can not move one second without the power of "Energy" within your body. Your body depends upon "Energy" for all of it's needs. Not only your human body, but the trees, grass, insects, animals, the stars, galaxies, planets etc. all depend upon "Energy" for it's daily life. Why? Because "Energy" is Life and life never, ever, never ever, never ever dies. What religion call the soul, spirit and mind is nothing but "Energy' called by another name. This is why Environment al Education is so crucial, with out it the world population is totally lost and can not really understand why thy exist on the planet earth in the first place. Environmental knowledge is the highest knowledge in Creation because it constantly evolves, expand, accelerate, elaborate on all things in Creation and it is superior intelligence to any knowledge in Creation. All Religions are man made and could never equal the knowledge of the Natural Environment. Having said that, we must now turn our attention to our next level and focus, where do we go when we leave our bodies and exit the Planet Earth? If we never truly understand how the particulates work (those little small tiny elements), we can never understand how the "Energy "work within our own body until we understand those images within our dreams during our sleep. We can see our loved ones image in our dreams and in many cases we fine ourselves in situation that we dislike and "Energy" always come to the rescue and awaken us in time for our bodies come back to life, This is called O.B.E. or (Out of Body Experience) Many are practicing this each and every day. A person that practice Yoga does this quite often because they recognize that there is a higher knowledge than religion.

We the People of The United States

Mr. President:

We the People of the United States of America see what is happening to you and your Administration and we think it is about time that drastic measures are taken to stop this vast insidious, recalcitrant and recidivist behavior subjected upon you and your family. We know that there is a great amount of fear that is imposed upon you because of your ethnicity. We recognize how you addresses Former President George W. Bush and Vice President Dick Chenney when the evidence was clear that these two individuals was not charged with ***Criminal War Crimes*** for invading Iraq even though there was clear evidence of their crimes. We know that The Rich and Wealthy Slave Masters are behind your fears because they are also responsible for getting you elected as President of the United States. ***We know th.at you are not blind to these facts.*** Material wealth is the true God in American life. less you forget who put you in power. The right to vote is nothing but a fasud orchestrated by the Rich and Wealthy Slave Masters to make it appear that the people are the ones that elect the President. How is this so when the electoral college is operative power that elects the President of the United States? Mr. President, You need to take some drastic actions so that the American people will have some sort of security in America. This week is the 50th Anniversary of Civil Rights Act of 1964. Dr. King made his "I Have A Dream Speech" and the March on Washington. What good was the March on Washington when there was no action taken after the March? Reverend Laoury said it best:, "The more things change the more they remain the same". There are white supremacist in the State of Dakota developing a racist community for the purpose of instilling fear in the people. Lastly, The rich and wealthy want you to attack the people in Syria because they use chemical weapons on their people, But it was the Rich and Wealthy that orchestrated that whole conflict in Syria, Afghanistan, and Iraq. Racism is being taught in the Church's, synagogues and mosques all over the world as we speak. So who is fooling who? What are you going to do Mr. President?

Quantum Physics

Last Week the media profiled a young 11year old African American boy that was home schooled, graduated from high school at age 10 Magna Cum Laude and now entering college at age 11 with a major in "Quantum Physics". Let us look at this child as an outstanding achievement by his parents who had taught him well. How was this possible? *First, the parents believed in themselves that they could better teach their child and do a better job than the public school system*. According to the mother, the child was a typical little boy that wanted to learn and was veryobedient to his parents. This should tell us just how important home school can be if the parents was serious about educating their children seeing that the mother is the child's first teacher. Let us take this a little deeper. In my book "The Shocking", we talked about Molecules, what is a molecule? A molecule: "is an electrically neutral group of two or more <u>atoms</u> held together by a <u>chemical</u> bond." *Let us understand that this entire creation is a chemistryy*. When looking at molecules under a microscope we can see the movement of these molecules and all motion is produced by "Energy", As you watch these molecules enter act, you can see that they all are connected with each other and when other molecules enter act they form a bond or connection with each other. *This is why the body human is connected with each and every human being on the face of the earth. What hurts you, hurts me and what hurts me hurts you as we are all connected with each other.* When you learn Quantum Physics you learn how the whole of Creation is connected with each and everything in creation. Quantum also means to advance foreword, however, many of us have retrograded and we are moving backwards because our science teachings are about 15,000 years behind the times. Technology is nothing new to Creation, there are other forms of life in our solar system, the universe that has advanced technology a thousand times greater than what we have on earth. Just look at the UFOs that we can never bring to the forefront so that the people can see for themselves what going on in our universe. Have you ever heard of a person doing a "Quantum Leap"? Many call this OBE or (Out of Body Experience).go to Burt Goldman's web site and take a look at OBE, This is why Environmental Education is so important to the human mind.

OUT-OF-SIGHT, OUT-OF-MIND

What does it mean when we say: ***"OUT-OF-SIGHT, OUT-OF-MIND"***? It means that those things that are not visible to the physical eye or conscious to the mental sight of the human mind, you can not see what is actually happening all around you. If you ca n not see what is being said with your physical eye sight or conscious of what is going on around you, you are totally oblivious as to what is truly happening in your own environment. Please do not feel that you are alone in this way of thinking, there are billions of people all around the world that thinks in this fashion. How can we improve from this way of thinking? We must start looking within our own mind as to what we are thinking about and how we think. Many of us still have sex on the brain, drugs, alcohol, sports, politices, religion etc. ***When you look at this vast creation this alone should tell you that there are things much greater than the everyday things we are so obsessed about***. First, let us look at the suffering President Obama is going through. Congress wont support any thing President Obama propose, The Republican Party want to shut down the government and appeal Obama Care that is already the law of the land. These idiots will say no to anything President Obama will support. ***This is the true practice, ce of racism at the highest level of government***. These individual in Congress don't care about democracy, they only care about enslavement of themasses, and how much money they can acquire in the process. But, if you ask them if they are believers in Christianity they will agree whole heatedly and that they are Christians and this is how religion has influenced this maddest on those who believe in religion and it does not matter what religion they believe in, the whole religious system is dysfunctional and corrupt . . . Look what religion is doing to the people in Syria, Afghanistan Iraq, Iran, India China etc. The Rich is getting Richer and the poor is getting poorer. ***All around the world the same song***.

Environmental Education Is Absent From the Curriculum of Knowledge

Environmental Education has been absent from the curriculum of knowledge for a very long time and the proof is in the behaviors of the people around the world. If a person do not understand the workings of the environment, they are totally lost from the reality of the environment. This go's back to the OUT-OF-SIGHT, OUT-OF-MIND SYNDROM. The workings of "Energy" is the main factor. The positive and negative "Energies" contribute to the causes of violence that has become so potent in our society? The molecules, particulates and bacteria is a part of this working environment and is very active within the human body. Most of us just shrug it off and say the people is just crazy and mad. Environmental Education was denied to the masses for good reasons. When you remove the environmental education from the curriculum component of learning you in fact deny the people the benefits of a true and well rounded education. There was a substitute for environmental education that dates back hundreds of years, which makes it so difficult for people to understand what has happen to them. There is a very good reason why science and religion does not mix. The science of the natural environment is in conflict with religious beliefs and this is where environmental education has been denied to the masses worldwide.

We Cannot Advance To Our Future by Cling to Our Past

If we continue to cling to our past we will never advance to our future. Additionally, if you don't know your past, how can you know your future. If you examine the United States Constitution as an example of past information not conducive to today's times in our own life time. We can see that the language in this document does not apply to this day and time. However our government continues to use this document as a point of referencewhen the focus is on our democracy. The Clergy in all religions has this same problem when they reference their beliefs in the bible and their terminology of God as a Savior. What is more important is "What are they being saved from? ***Today on the news a Deacon in a church and friend to a Pastor some where down in Louisiana walked into the church with a shot gun and shot the Preacher twice at point blank range because the Preacher had sex with the Deacon's wife and according to the broadcast, this same Preacher had sex with the Deacon's daughter and she was found pregnant. Additionally, this Minister also was having sex with other members of his congregation.*** This Preacher is not alone in his sexual aggressions with his congregation. Reverend Jesse L. Jackson was having sex with a member of his congregation and this woman got pregnant by Reverend Jackson and was allowed to sleep at his house and was a friend to Reverend Jackson's wife. Reverend Larry King was found having sex with young boys at his church and the list goes on and on. Yet the congregation continue to believe in religious gossip, garbage in garbage out. There are many more ministers in all denominations practice illicit sexual behavior, There is the Catholic Church that is known for its practices of pedophilia with young under age boys, then there are the Muslims that rape young girls and this beat goes on and on. In religion there are billions of men women and children that keep this practice going on in a secret and clandestine manner so that others will never know whats going on. This not only happens in churches it happen with members of your own families incest is nothing knew, the slave masters of yesterday and today still utilize incest as a personal secret from society and other family members. The Slave Master enjoyed the Practice of the Mandingo men mating with young slave girls to produce more slaves, the

Slave Master would equally enjoy watching the young son from the womb of his own mother who gave him birth have sex with his own mother to produce more slaves for himself. ***Religion is what produce these practices and this is what we are retrograding back to. When you practice religion you are truly practicing a sinister belief in something you have no idea of what you are doing.***

Government Shutdown is Equal to Extortion and Blackmail

Mr. President:

Why has not Eric Holder the Attorney General of the United States made an arrest to those Congressional individuals that have committed _**Extortion and Blackmail**_ against the President of the United States by Shutting down the Government?? _**Is the United States Congress above the law?**_ Extortion and blackmail are similar in concept in violation of _**Title 18 USC 871-873 of the Criminal Code**_, but there are differences between the two. Extortion is a form of theft that occurs when an offender obtains money, property, or _**services**_ from another person through coercion. To constitute coercion, the necessary act can be the threat of violence, destruction of property, or imp Extortion is a crime in which one person forces another person to do something against his will, generally to give up money or other property, by threat of violence, property damage, and damage to the person's reputation, or extreme financial hardship. Extortion involves the victim's consent to the crime, but that consent is obtained illegally. Roper government action. Inaction of the testimony or the withholding of testimony in a legal action Current through Pub. L. 113-36. (See Public Laws for the current Congress.)

(a) Whoever knowingly and willfully deposits for conveyance in the mail or for a delivery from any post office or by any letter carrier any letter, paper, writing, print, missive, or document containing any threat to take the life of, to kidnap, or to inflict bodily harm upon the President of the United States, the President-elect, the Vice President or other officer next in the order of succession to the office of President of the United States, or the Vice President-elect, or knowingly and willfully otherwise makes any such threat against the President, President-elect, Vice President or other officer next in the order of succession to the office of President, or Vice President-elect, shall be fined under this title or imprisoned not more than five years, or both.

(b) The terms "President-elect" and "Vice President-elect" as used in this section shall mean such persons as are the apparent successful candidates for the offices of President and Vice President, respectively, as ascertained from the results of the general elections held to determine the electors of President and Vice President in accordance with title 3, United States Code, sections 1 and 2. The phrase "other officer next in the order of succession to the office of President" as used in this section shall mean the person next in the order of succession to act as President in accordance with title 3, United States Code, sections 19 and 20.are also acts that constitute coercion. As a theft crime, extortion is often graded as a felony or a misdemeanor depending on the amount of money or the value of the property or services extorted from the victim.

18 USC 873—Blackmail

U.S. Code > Title 18 > Part I > Chapter 41 > § 873—Blackmail

Current as of: February 2010
Check for updates

Whoever, by force, intimidation, or threat of procuring dismissal from employment, or by any other manner whatsoever induces any person employed in the construction, prosecution, completion or repair of any public building, public work, or building or work financed in whole or in part by loans or grants from the United States, to give up any part of the compensation to which he is entitled under his contract of employment, shall be fined under this title or imprisoned not more than five years, or both.

Legislative History

Here is a Fact that Can Never be Disputed

Here is a fact that can never be disputed. The human creation went through a chemistry process in the womb of science before arriving here on earth in this environment. Scientology tried to integrate science with religion, and fail drastically. Remember, religion is only a theory and will always be just a theory.

Communication is the Highest Educational form of Teaching in all Creation

Communication is truly the highest educational form of teaching in all of Creation, even a person totally blind or deaf and can't hear can communicate with those that cannot see or hear. When a person open their eyes after a nights sleep, their eyes communicate with all that's in their sight. in the open environment there are trees, grass, the natural environment, your eyes telecommunication with every single thing within the sight of your eyes. Your eyes, ears, nose, mouth and your senses are the communication apparatus to all that you come in contact with. When you look at your automobile you are communicating with an animated object, the car can only move when you ignite the engine and give it "Energy" that makes it move. That same "Energy" is the same apparatus that cause the human body to breath, to talk, to walk, to run, to think etc. The human body cannot think for itself, it takes "Energy" to think, the human body and all of its blood and organs are only the vehicle for the use of "Energy". At the time of your death, your body will loose all of its "Energy" unless "Energy" decide to allow you a reprieve for a few more days or years. Most people say that you cheated death. No, you cannot cheat death, when your time is up, nothing can bring you back. Death itself is nothing more than a product of "Energy" and the term is use to identify the end of life and is the transport to and from one dimension to the next dimension or environment. The environment is perpetual; in each and every dimension the environment is different. And "Energy" is always working in each and every dimension; thereby when your "Energy" exits from your body death transport that "Energy" to its next destination where ever that may be. Please keep in mind that "Energy" is life and life is "Energy" the creator of all things in this Universe and all the other Universes in Creation. Your death is not your first death; you are like a traveler passing through this planet call earth.

Domestic Violence is a Serious Health Hazard

Domestic violence has always been a serious health hazard among women and men for centuries but very seldom addressed in the eyes of health care enthusiast or the media, it has always been an act of clandestine practice. This act of violence began in the minds of many dysfunctional behavioral men and women; however, the majority of these acts are by misguided male individuals with a propensity to act aggressively toward women and young children with low self-esteem. The meaning of violence is the threat to harm yourself or another by force. However, it began to formulate in the mind by negative forces or thoughts of violent behavior. It is truly a heath care disparity among the majority of women who become afraid to voice their opinion on this subject in fear of reprisal from friends or foe. Today is a new day to awaken our thoughts to that higher "Energy" within you, that is telling you that there is something much greater than what has been happening to you, your children and family? Domestic violence is akin to a drug addict that needs a fix but don't have the money to get it. Or when they do get it, violence become a sexual perversion for aggressive and violent behavior, with many men, they actually acquire a physical erection in their penis just thinking about violent aggressive behavior. You might find this kind of behaviors in penal institutions among men and women. Like HIV-AIDS and other communicable diseases if this behavior is not treated within the penal institutions, this behavior will follow that individual out of prison and into the families in their own communities. Then the community becomes infected by this disease of dysfunctional behavior.

Are We Truly Robotic Creatures?

"Energy" is the true Source Code for all data and life in Creation. A robot is a mechanical or virtual agent, usually an electro-mechanical machine that is guided by a computer program or electronic circuitry. "Energy" being the Source Code suggests that "Energy" is also computerized, otherwise, how could we have ever developed the computer? Robots can be autonomous or semi-autonomous and range from humanoids such as Honda's Advanced Step in Innovative Mobility (ASIMO) and TOSY's TOSY Ping Pong Playing Robot (TOPIO) to industrial robots, collectively programmed 'swarm' robots, and even microscopic Nano robots. By mimicking a lifelike appearance or automating movements, a robot may convey a sense of intelligence or thought of its own. When death approaches us, all "Energy" exits the body and the body is buried in the ground or cremated. But, what happen to that "Energy" that left that body? It returns to that Source that Created that body through a system of high powered Chemistry.

Robotics is the branch of technology that deals with the design, construction, operation, and application of robots, [2] as well as computer systems for their control, sensory feedback, and information processing. These technologies deal with automated machines that can take the place of humans in dangerous environments or manufacturing processes, or resemble humans in appearance, behavior, and/or cognition. Many of today's robots are inspired by nature contributing to the field of bio-inspired robotics. A Humanoid is like a human being in appearance 1. (Social Science / Anthropology & Ethnology) a being with human rather than anthropoid characteristics, 2. (Literary & Literary Critical Terms) (in science fiction) a robot or creature resembling a human being. A creature resembling man, as one of man's early ancestors.

Politics & Religion is the worse forms of Enslavement

Look at the meanings of these two words and judge for yourself, they are design to control the mind set of the masses.

The word **Politics is taken** (from <u>Greek</u>: *politikos*, meaning "of, for, or relating to citizens") is the practice and theory of influencing other people on a civic or individual level. More narrowly, it refers to achieving and exercising positions of <u>governance</u>—organized control over a human community, particularly a <u>state</u>. A variety of methods are employed in politics, which include promoting its own political views among people, <u>negotiation</u> with other political subjects, making <u>laws</u>, and exercising <u>force</u>, including <u>warfare</u> against adversaries. Politics is exercised on a wide range of social levels, from <u>clans</u> and<u>tribes</u> of traditional societies, through modern <u>local governments</u>, <u>companies</u> and institutions up to <u>sovereign states</u>, to <u>international level</u>.

A <u>political system</u> is a framework which defines acceptable political methods within a given society. <u>History of political thought</u> can be traced back to early antiquity, with seminal works such as <u>Plato</u>'s *Republic*, <u>Aristotle</u>'s *Politics* and opus of <u>Confucius</u>.

The word **Religion** is an organized collection of <u>beliefs</u>, <u>cultural systems</u>, and <u>world views</u> that relate humanity to an order of existence.[note 1] Many religions have <u>narratives</u>, <u>symbols</u>, and <u>sacred histories</u> that are intended to explain the <u>meaning of life</u>and/or to explain the <u>origin of life</u> or the <u>Universe</u>. From their beliefs about the <u>cosmos</u> and <u>human nature</u>, people derive<u>morality</u>, <u>ethics</u>, <u>religious laws</u> or a preferred <u>lifestyle</u>. According to some estimates, there are roughly 4,200 religions in the world.[1]

Many religions may have organized <u>behaviors</u>, <u>clergy</u>, a definition of what constitutes adherence or membership, <u>holy places</u>, and <u>scriptures</u>. The practice of a religion may also include <u>rituals</u>, <u>sermons</u>, commemoration or veneration of a <u>deity</u>, <u>gods</u> or<u>goddesses</u>, <u>sacrifices</u>, <u>festivals</u>, <u>feasts</u>, <u>trance</u>, <u>initiations</u>, <u>funerary services</u>, <u>matrimonial services</u>, <u>meditation</u>, <u>prayer</u>, <u>music</u>, art, dance, public service or other aspects of human culture. Religions may also contain mythology.[2]

The word *religion* is sometimes used interchangeably with *faith*, *belief system* or sometimes *set of duties*;[3] however, in the words of Émile Durkheim, religion differs from private belief in that it is "something eminently social".[4] A global 2012 poll reports that 59% of the world's population is religious, and 36% are not religious, including 13% who are atheists, with a 9 percent decrease in religious belief from 2005.[5] On average, women are more religious than men.[6] Some people follow multiple religions or multiple religious principles at the same time, regardless of whether or not the religious principles they follow traditionally allow for syncretism.

The Power of Creation

Did you know that Creation moves at a speed higher and faster than light, thought, warp speed combine? Let us kick this up a notch. It is Creation that causes change as things are changing right before our eyes even faster than we can ever comprehend, at every fraction of a second and sooner. Our days are passing at a high rate of speed and when we reflect this movement we are in ah. Check this out. The earth is spinning at one thousand miles an hour and it makes a complete revolution within 24 hour or less. This means in the course of one day the earth has traveled about 24,000 miles. *__That is extremely fast. Yet, if there are any elements, such as neutrons, electrons, protons photons etc. or any other particulates in the path of "Energy" as it is creating, it will be part of what ever is being Created at that time along with anything else in its path.__* Many times human birth does not produce the special child we would like and that child might arrive with deformity on multiple births. Example, should a woman give birth to sextuplets this implies that the sperm cell will quadruple in the ovum as part of that Creation of the fetus causing multiple births in the womb. Another example is that animals could arrive with deformity, In the news last week there was a cow that gave birth to a two headed calf causing that same principle to apply. We can no longer rely upon our political leaders and the clergy to teach our children the true essence of what we were sent here to do. It is time for us to take responsibility for our own research and intelligence. *__Each one of us were Created with our own genius, try seeking and searching for your own.__*

Nothing in all Creation can move without the Power of "Energy"

"Energy" is the guiding force for all things in motion and those things not in motion. This means that Nothing, absolutely nothing can move without the power of "Energy". All planets rotate by the power of "Energy". even inanimate things cannot remain stable except by the power of "Energy" who Created it. Should it be demolished it cannot remain stable except by the power of "Energy". ***A mountain cannot stand except by the power of "Energy" that created those lofty structures***. Most people have no idea what ***LIFE*** really is and what it means. ***"Energy" is Life and Life is "Energy" and "Energy" never, ever dies.*** "Energy" utilize the human, animal and insect corpse as a means to acknowledge it's presents and existence. This implies that "Energy" and life is every where in Creation even in our own universe and beyond. ***This also implies that yes, there is life on other planets not necessarily human but life or "Energy" as we know it to be,*** "Energy" is the anchor of all movements in Creation. This also implies that all knowledge is controlled by "Energy" because all knowledge has movement in all levels of communication and intelligence. ***"Energy" is the archives of all knowledge, wisdom and understanding in all Creation.*** Just look at your human body, nothing in it can move without: Energy" giving it the power to move. At the time of your death all movements will stop and your corpse will lay empty void of life and all movement. What happen to that vibrant life that was inside that body? Death another component of "Energy" causes that life to be transported to its next destination. This process and movements continues on into infinity. ***The "Energy" that was assign to you has traveled through this same procedure countless of centuries and times before, this is why you should never be afraid of death because you have died countless of times before.***

Female of the First Power in Human Creation

The woman is a true scientist by nature she is the female of the first Power in Human Creation. Why and How is this when most people that practice religious theology believe that the man created the woman from the rib of the male species. If this is what your religion teaches you and you believe that then you can keep on believing that animated fairy tale. This kind of foolishness that was made up by the idiots of religion long ago does not have any inkling of sound intelligence to say the lease and not one them even today can explain that none sense. ***The woman on the other hand has all the facts that suggest it was she the female that Created the male species and all facts support these findings. The woman carries both 'X' and 'Y' chromosome as she can give birth to both male and female.*** How is this done? ***Science has known that the female sea horse can give birth without the aid of the male.*** Most people believe that Mermaids are fictional creatures with no originality, and was replaced by fairy tales. Hidden knowledge makes it very difficult for the masses to ever comprehend what has happen over the centuries of time and replaced with fairy tales like Santa Claus, Red Riding Hood, Easter with a chicken egg, Jesus rising from the dead in three days after his death, the Son of God, etc., all fairy tales for the ignorant miss guided masses who has chosen religion for their knowledge and guide in understanding Creation. Nevertheless, there is a part of the female cultural history that has never been told to the human species and for good reason. As we reflect on the history of the woman, she was the first to become a slave for the male gender, she became personal property for the male. But at what point did all this take place? Why was she hated by the male species? Even today she is not allowed to be equal to our male counter part. In reality, the male envied her and wanted her power. The woman is the true homosexual by nature as she is a very extraordinary creature with extraordinary Power.

When the Mind Entertains Garbage it Becomes Addicted to That Garbage

When we speak of Garbage what does this really mean? The dictionary describes garbage as: Garbage thinking is like taking drugs or any other addictive behaviors it is worthless, useless, or unwanted matter. Also called: **rubbish** discarded or waste matter; refuse, informal nonsense, computing—invalid . Any matter that is no longer wanted or needed;trash, worthless talk; lies; foolishness. Anything that is <u>contemptibly</u> worthless, inferior, or vile. Probably from Anglo-French*garbelage* removal of discarded matter, of uncertain origin; compare Old Italian *garbuglio* confusion. We are constantly entertaining the use of Garbage each and every day, just look at our Educational System in America. ***Our children are constantly digesting Garbage on a daily bases because they are not given "Environmental Education" that is needed for the science of today***. Our children set in a class room all day reading books and at the end of the semester they are given a test concerning what they have read. Never taken out of the class room to study the environment where they live which is crucial for the development of the human mind and brain. ***These children will graduate from colleges and universities without a "environmental education," the only thing the child understands is the addiction of the Garbage that they have been taught, garbage in-garbage out.*** If we do not understand what the elements in the environment is doing to us on a daily bases we are living in a docile world of total ignorance.

A Typhon and Hurricane is One and The Same

The Typhoon in the Philippines is a very tragic and horrific situation, what was it that cause this catastrophe upon those people? Science is a beautiful thing once it is understood, but when we ignore science then we can be sure that a calamity can erupt within our own community. Here is the question, Who decide where a Typhoon or Hurricane should stick? Most people would say only God knows. Right? Each and everything in Creation was meant for you and I to know and there is nothing out of your reach for knowledge if you seek it. NOTHING! It is imperative that we learn the workings of the "Environment" at the highest level. It is "Energy" that causes these calamities as Typhon or Hurricanes are just one of the many arsenals of "Energy". _**Can we bring these calamities upon ourselves as a people?**_ The native Indians in America believed strongly that they could bring about rain when it was needed for their crops, so they did the "Rain Dance" and the rain came at the time they needed it. This is to say when the mind set of the people began to pool their thinking on one accord things can and will happen. When we summon "Energy" to come to us it will come at a time of great need and when it arrives it can be devastating to that people. _**That "Energy" within each and every human being is the same "Energy" that cause Typhoons and Hurricanes and has that same power to summon that great mountain of "Energy" that will come at a speed so powerful that it can demolish any and everything in its path. as it did in the Philippines**_. If the people do not understand science, how can they ever understand the environment where they live?

All Men are "NOT" Created Equal

Dear Mr. President:

I think you should take a step back and analyze what the "Bill of Rights" is truly saying that *"All men are Created Equal"*. There is no way a man could be equal to the next man their blood type could be different, the amount of blood could be different, their heads are different sizes as their hearts, lungs etc. If this was so, all the wealth of the world would be distributed equally and that is an impossibility. Do you actually believe that Warren Buffet or Bill Gates would give you half of their wealth so that you would become equals to them? That is truly crazy talk. I think that the so call Founding Fathers wanted to say that: *"All men **might** become equals* and **might** is the operative word and not that they are equals, and keep in mind that when this document was written, the men that wrote it had slaves and wealth. ***So how was it that the slave was equal to the Master?***

The Woman is The Kunapha, The High Priestess

What happen that the woman lost her power as the Kunapha or High Priestess? She lost the power when she was disconnected from the Cosmos as she fail from power and became the slave to the power of man. What does the word Cosmos mean?

The word derives from the Greek t

The Ancient and Medieval cosmos as depicted in Peter Apian's *Cosmographia* (Antwerp, 1539).

Cosmos is the Universe regarded as an ordered system.[1]erm κόσμος (*kosmos*), literally meaning "order" or "ornament" and metaphorically "world",[2] and is antithetical to the concept of chaos. Today, the word is generally used as a synonym of the Latin loanword "Universe" (considered in its orderly aspect). The word cosmetics originates from the same root. In many Slavic languages such as Russian, Polish, Bulgarian, and Serbian, the word *kosmos* (**космос**) also means "outer space".

When the woman was disconnected from that order of the Cosmos something drastic happen to her. What was It? When the woman created the male species and taught him how to become human, she gave him the power to subdue her natural order, consequently causing her natural power to erode from her. But how did this happen? Man discovered that if he could develop a reasonable convincing source that the woman could follow he could take her power and control her by forces unknown to her. At this point in history "Religion" was born. The woman never lost her power to create and give birth as the male species knew that the woman was the reproductive mechanism for his future children. Today we can now see why the male has treated her so cruel over the centuries. She has become the wicked witch, a voo doo curse, a slave and personal property for the male species. She can never have as much wealth and power as the male as long as the male has the wealth and power over the female. Here is the question: When and at what point will the woman reclaim her status and power as the High Priestess? ***She can never re-claim her power so long as she practice the man made Religions.*** The Woman has the natural ability to bring order from chaos.

About the Author

If you have an open mind and are seeking a much higher level of understanding the environment this book is for you. This book is for those who are environmentally conscience. The author, Charles Fletcher wrote several articles in an attempt to change the thinking and thought process of all those who read this book. It is his hope that each and everyone that reads this book will be able to see what the author has seen by turning their attention inward to show how our thoughts and the process of thought really works. The author believes that our public schools and many universities have never taught this imperative subject. This book will definitely show you how and what to look for.